cups in the cupboard

cups in the cupboard

by clarissa r. sutton

ISBN: 979-8-9907012-0-5

crsutton.com

for everyone who taught me poetry,
including those who taught me how to love,
and how to love myself

I drank some milk,
I said goodbye,
I went up in
the early sky.

~Clarissa, age 4

cups, in the cupboard

there are
drinking glasses, packed
into the shelves of my ribcage—
mugs that fall out and
shatter when I breathe too deeply,
everyday misery seeping all
over the floor.
champagne flutes rattle, too high up
for me to reach. I've lost access
to soft relief, while
plastic colored cups filled with watery lemonade
for the backyard summer potluck
spill
shots of whisky
and false hope
lining the bones of my hips.
I dig out cracked teacups
from my spine and pray the peace
doesn't drizzle out too fast, stumbling over
discarded bottles that crumble
beneath my broken feet. I cage handmade
coffee cups full of carefully
constructed empathy deep behind the bars,
afraid of what will happen
if I let
these feelings show.

poetry
   is the crack
         that
   lets
         the
light
   in

coffee

1. longing

anticipation always comes before
the fall, sweet—like vanilla, or wishes made
on a birthday cake: desires that never truly satisfy,
but I still won't let them go. I pick the fruit too soon,

just barely, enough to make the bitter linger
on my tongue. I ignore it, for now, and try
to tread carefully. somehow, I still manage
to burn myself anyway, eager for what once
I avoided so particularly. Is this fleeting
excitement in my shaky veins a smile
put on for show? back when wearing
mismatched shoes was cool and we
ignored deep questions and bad hair
I now reject the acrid loneliness in the
empty grounds, throw myself into the
unending question of a shooting star

and pray i didn't give away the only un-
decaying piece left inside my heart

study of 38hz in 600nm

my veins shudder with fire, warning lights
that flash on the fronts of cars
careening down the brick alley inside my mind;
bright signs precede construction
around every turn.
(there is always construction here.)
this sidewalk is littered with thoughts that
have lost their potency—
cigarette butts
scattered in the cracks, saggy jack-o-lanterns left out in
the frost, (weathered paint lines)

"No Street Crossing At This Time"
says the LED hand, above the crosswalk,
but my feet don't stop moving
through the amber memories of honey tinted sky
candles glowing in the dark,
casting caramel colored ruddiness
over the marigold dreams hidden inside,
the sharp taste of ginger trembling
on my tongue,
instead of gentle apricot (instead of
kind peach, instead of
witty mango) when I speak.

monarch butterflies migrate
to the inside of my chest, while clownfish swim
the length of my bones, their fluttering fins leave
terracotta stains behind,
so that rust and clay fall from my open hands
onto tiger lilies, (onto Anthony Eden tulips),
staining the sunset,
causing autumn oak and maple trees to
cast fragmented bronze light on my tired words,
and flashing neon lights leave the residue
of a melted cream sickle
on my skin.

urgency of an echo

In the morning, I wake early and drink
hot coffee, bitter and dark to clear the echo
left inside my mind from dreams that wish to insult
all progress I made last night, with calm
visions of my future. Instead, I wake cross
and crabby, hoping some of it will stay.

There is nothing here that begs me to stay,
I am left in a world where the drink
on my lips could condemn me to a cross
the richness of wine in my throat a mere echo
to what I might find amidst a quiet calm
meant to keep me safe, rather than insult

I find these words at the base of my skull, screaming
insult after insult but I choose to keep my voice down, to
stay and fight for the overwhelming calm
that all too soon will crash over me, fill my drink
with a sense of quiet, lose the urgency in an echo
until I almost forget that I once was cross.

Winter comes too quickly, but don't cross
the river until it is fully frozen, lest a careless insult
cracks the ice and you are left to echo
the shattering ice in your bones. No, stay
and dine with me, have a drink
and you can go when the storm is calm.

Will my chest ever again find its calm?
Don't mistake my longing as an invitation to cross
into this world I've created, don't drink
to my good health, for that would insult
the way you couldn't be compelled to stay
and soon will be nothing but an empty echo.

When I look at the stars, I feel them echo
my heart, in the waves of the ocean, calm
and broad, asking you to stay, please stay.
But perhaps this is the way I bear my cross
(though that metaphor is not meant to insult)
perhaps of my own downfall I will drink

and in the deep echo, the ferrymen cross
the river, collect their calm with an open insult:
maybe I'll ask you to stay for just one more drink

tapestry of time

there is no such thing
as time as we think of it,
at least according to physics.
Which means,
I guess,
that (lack of) time is irrelevant
when it comes to me and you.
Maybe I'm getting ahead of myself
(but then again, maybe not).
Because if time is a network
of connections spread out
(like space)
and intertwined in a tapestry
then maybe
I can believe in love (at first sight).
And if, in this infinite dimensional space,
we are the only things
that assign those threads meaning
who's to say
that I'm not already connected to you
from now until forever-
both the way that I'm connected
to the rest of the universe,
and in a way that is
blindingly, (indubitably,) unique?

peace in mediocrity

good days
are the very first
sip of coffee, burning
the tip of my tongue:
hopeful anticipation
crumbled in haste,

motion, converging
with stillness:
the way
everything spins too fast
when the train
comes to a stop.

bad days
slink between the
sheets and fill my ears
with cotton, darkness
in my lungs spilling
out like tar at night

without it
I feel hollow,
but the pressure
inside is not sure if
it's meant to cave in
or explode

Seasonal Affects

the problem,
of course,
is not that the air is too dry

rather

craggy branches beckon the swollen sky, stretching their
fingers up until
the ice coats their
bare bones,
                    grasping
at the clouds, clawing for crumbs
       of moisture
to fill the air

the river dawdles.
in this cold softness,
city noise muffled by a shroud of conjugal rice
       that tumbles
          down,
               down,
                    down.
the problem,

of course,
is not that the clouds glow orange,
filling the streets with
bright darkness,

heavy cotton lingering here
because it has nowhere else to go,
filling the streets
until the whole world is swaddled, at rest.

the problem,

       of course

is that,
       in the morning,
salt and crystals
shatter the softness
       weighing on the ground
       mixing into sludge and clogging
           the arteries, wet cement
               slopping on and sticking
                  to everything, leaving
               behind chalky remains.

The Problem, of course, is not
that the air is too dry, rather,
that the dryness comes after the flood,

and when it does dry up, it dries too quickly.

light pollution

weathered bones hum with grief,
creaking their joints against the night sky.
darkness doesn't fill the air here—
it's much too bright in city bounds.

I used to be afraid of an orange sky:
the sign of something bad to come.
this is not a disaster, though: just clouds
lining the atmosphere. even without them,

light still blocks the cosmic view,
constricting us until we are merely
ants on the ground, surrounded
by stomping skyscrapers,

walls of apartment buildings
closing in until breathing
stale air feels normal, and
the grittiness of concrete beneath

our feet becomes the natural walking path.
I reach for smells of car exhaust
and cigarette smoke, fishing them out
of my pockets like train tickets,

ride the grid between the buildings
forget the veins scattered across the
countryside that used to call my name,
find comfort in light from windows

instead of endless stars.

empath

it is not as generous as
it seems the bones
in my chest

shatter

as they try to wrap around
your heart there's not enough room
in here

for the two of us but damn it

i'll try

(even if i have to
                    shove
                            myself
                                    aside.)

emptiness

emptiness arrives early,
bare soles pressed
to the cold bathroom tile
on a winter morning.
grey light filtering
across white walls
patterns of reminiscence
dripping into the sink

the plants are withering.
it's probably too cold
for them here. or maybe
they didn't get enough water.
the lack of sun doesn't
help much either,
so they sit alone
and shrivel and fade.

irrational

I stand in the kitchen
at 6:23
AM, struck with a sudden
jolt
of fear
because I'm not wearing
a seatbelt.
instinct is a funny thing—
sudden impulses
in my brain screaming
Something
Is
Wrong!
grasping for the first
measure of safety
it can
find to keep me
safe

crevices

i.
everybody dies alone, they say, but
its not the dying that scares me.

ii.
I only remember you in bright soccer socks,
sliding down the empty hallways after school:
your laugh was contagious, and now

you send me drunk snapchats on New Years
as the very first indication that
dying's not what scares you, either.

iii.
what happens when the world becomes too much?
when the brick pavement below is a
better place to lie
than a pillow on a bed?

when the bottle I decide to drink is
made of propionic acid instead of ethanol

and I paint my wrists with silver
lines that turn my skin to red?

iv.
loneliness is the cracks between bricks on
the apartment wall across from my window.

I've mostly come to peace with myself inside,
fragile though it may be.
I can only hope the same for you.

v.
we meet for coffee,
all I can see are the crevices
you've tried to disguise as a wall, the scaffolding
in the kitchen
holding up pieces of our hearts that are unsure
of where to go, trying to keep
our walls from shattering
in the rain.

Season of Lassitude

"Nature likes to hide itself"
        ~Heraclitus

Apathy creeps inside the seams of my clothing
hiding grumpy Monday mornings
in the pockets of my coat for me to
find like a five dollar bill:
stashed and forgotten.
(Somehow, this indifference
is a much less welcome gift.)

Autumn rain fills my boots
with cold promises of winter, and
I find bitterness like morning frost
creeping onto the edges of
my attitude, snarky comments falling
as quickly as the trees undress,
cloudy skies stopping the humor from
crunching happily beneath my shoes.

The tiles of my shower wall
hold exhaustion in their grout lines
and lukewarm water beats
a staccato pulse of boredom
on my shoulders, doing its best to
keep the anxiety still curled up under
my comforter from waking. Still, I wash
my hair with impudence to prepare
for when it does.

Afterward, rising panic in my coffee mug
warms my hands and jump-starts
my heart, but does nothing to keep the
plants on the windowsill from drooping
as I flip through emotions like old
photographs until faded ink is
all that remains, the carafe in my chest
sitting empty and unused.

(I'll probably find more apathy in
my coat pockets tomorrow morning.)

mid-urban daydreams

rubber runs rampant on
                              these cold concrete streets:
             car tire residue
                    leaving smudges like the black
                    nail polish spilling from a
                                          hard
                                                empty
                                                        bottle
                             that I keep to write
                    letters
                    on the backs
                    of my library receipts,
                             that I keep to spin tales:
                    of an elf
                          lost at sea;
                    of fairies revered
                          for courage and loyalty.
             instead,
                    my shoes squelch in the mush left
                    on the sidewalk,
                    I jerk awake to the smell of ground pepper
                          Sea salt left on my lips,
and I walk away,
                    blind
                             to the broken world around
                    me.

26

hours of darkness

in the middle of the night i wake and
realize the toothpaste has run out,
cold fear tethering me to the sheets.
they are dark against my rattling knuckles,
muscles cramped from the strain of my grip.

i shove plants into every corner
of the kitchen cupboard, overflow it with
dying life. the viper's bowstring is turning
brown. geranium leaves litter the floor:
the flower buds left a long time ago.

gravel roads slink through the darkness,
rattling cars drive way too fast, mile after
mile. i find my way home, to the floor of my
bedroom, hands reach behind for my shoulder
blades, and let the walls of my ribs cave in.

to atone

a·tone /əˈtōn/
    verb.
        to make amends or reparation.

I wrote penance on my skin
to absolve myself of sin—
I hoped that if I tore the flesh
above my ribs, that the darkness
would bleed out and I'd be free

maybe if I dig deep
enough, I can rip off my skin, s
hed this empty carcass for
a new one, curl up like death
or maybe birth.

tea

2. loving

I left the peaches out to rot, forgetting that, when left too
long, fruit will over-ripen. left like green leaves, turning
bitter in the bag, steeped too hot, burning my mouth. It's an
addiction
I cannot break, trying to fit myself into new flavors with
the strainer, hoping that i'll find the right combination
of temperature and honey to keep me satisfied. I
hold on with reddened palms, pretend that a
steaming mug is an acceptable substitute
for another hand in mine, sticky sweet
Steam rising from the drink,
a ritualistic obsession
creeping from the kettle on the stove.
I'm always left wanting more—hoping it will fill the void
inside, hoping this fixation will force the cosmic hand, or at
least distract me from impending pain. I'll do it differently
next time, I hope, but for now, the china cup on the counter
grows cold, and I wonder: is this what it's like to forget to
remember to live?

(some)day

sunrise
shatters the suspense. patterned
shadows on the wall of an
empty bedroom
cold covers crumpled, littered
across the floor.

a piece of my heart
will always belong to you.

winter chill

winter light is cold
and tired, leftover
      coffee grounds
scattered over the kitchen floor
      early in the morning.

we wrap ourselves in pretense
      to guard against the chill
and trip over shadows
      on the sidewalks
         in the sun.

wishing does not make it snow

the snow has fallen and melted,
and still I long for the snow,

—to step outside on Christmas Eve
into a world embraced in softness,
sparkling in warm yellow streetlight
in the car, after a candle lit service.

I want snow the way
the mountains want snow,
straightening their tired spines
to welcome gentle insulation,
a blanket of winter that brings
much-wanted visitors with it. I want snow

like a skier wants snow—without it they wait alone,
waxing their skis and longing to bundle up and
ride the lifts; pining for a dance with the mountain
in a spray of white powder, craving the push and pull of
moguls beneath their feet.

I want snow the way a winter February day wants snow.
It's too cold out,
but the flurries make it gentler. Somehow
the cold is worth it,
if there is only snow.

I want a blizzard.
All I've ever gotten was the shavings of ice
on an indoor skating rink.
I'd settle even for a layer of soft dust
covering the ground,
the type that is unsure if it will melt away or accumulate
more.

there are flurries in the air—I long to wake up tomorrow
to a snowball fight, to crunch along in my barely-used
winter boots, bundle in a heavy coat, with a crisp wind

nipping at my nose that makes blankets and tea
that much more welcome when returning home.
I want to catch the flakes on my tongue again,
carefree and childlike.

It's cloudy out, and so
I long for winter to be the way
it is supposed to be,
the way it was when I was young.
I long for hopeful, gentle, childlike joy;

but instead of snowmen and angels, you're building
sandcastles on the beach, and I watch them crumble in
the hot sun and wash away into the ocean the way I
should have expected you to walk away:

inevitably.

Stranger In A Burning House

I have traveled too long with insomnia
creeping like fire through my bones, the spark
in my veins a stray ember that rips through
gasoline and keeps me awake all night.
The damage is already done: I started falling
in love with you when I was only eight years old.

Maybe love is too strong a word. I was a child
with matches, lighting a candle just to watch it burn,
too young to understand how quickly a tiny flame can
turn into a roaring blaze, burning a jagged scar right
through
the middle of my heart, oxygen and heat and friction
turning the hardwood of the floors to ash.

Heat swelters through the crawl spaces in the attic
and the aorta in my chest, but even though it's burning,
it's never burning down—as a child, your house
was my favorite place to wake up: I dig a trench and fill
it with saltwater of sweat and tears, and pray
that when it burns, the fire won't touch mine.

But I can no longer see the forest, for the trees
are all ablaze. I see a stranger now, when I look
into your eyes, a charred skeleton—ash, metal, bone—
all that remains of a life we'll never know. I think
maybe I longed too much for a light that did not exist
instead of learning how to live without the flame.

Darling, we are made of subtleties that never line up
quite right, peeling paper on the wall that got too close
to the kerosene lamp. Smoke fills my lungs
and offers relief for my insomnia. You sneak into
my dreams, but when I wake, it's to an empty
house stripped bare, without a roof. I want to cling

to every smoldering ember I have left: I succeed only
in burning my palms as I try to rebuild. The difference
is, fires eventually burn out and I don't know how
to smother mine without smothering too much of me.
If it stays, I promise to keep it in a fireplace this time,
but when you leave, please take the insomnia too.

fly / fall

you were
my favorite cliffhanger:
I was so anxious
to see
what would happen next.

but.
we were children
when I fell in love
thinking that was all we needed.

it was
and it wasn't

all at the same time.

I am cold
all the time now,
hollowing of my bones
leaves only
lethargic recompense
for roadside blackbirds
to find.

quantum entanglement

some say soulmates contain
particles that were
entangled at the beginning
of the universe
once touching,
now scattered apart, across
space (and maybe time),
trying to find
their way back to each other.
I don't know if I believe
in soulmates, but I know
I do believe we were scattered
apart too soon, shattered
in the rapid expanse of something
neither of us knew how to explain.
I'm not saying I don't believe
in fate, some days I do,
and even if soulmates do exist
I don't know what that says
about us. because even if
they don't, I know that some
part of me will always be
tangled up in some
part of you

disposable

for here
　　　　or to go
we never asked often enough,
skinned knuckles
　　　　skittering
across the jawline of all my failed attempts
at any kind of relationship.
I should have been more clear from the start.
　　　　disposable
was never going to work
for me and you.

paper
　　　　hearts aren't strong enough
to keep out the cold, fresh
　　　　　　snow always a reminder of
how quickly our memories vanish,
　　　　muted
in the tongue-tied footsteps
　　　　on a hidden parking lot;
children shouldn't be allowed
to hang wishes from
　　　　　　the sky.

but you never apologized
　　　　　　for not loving me back.
and I always forget an extra travel mug
　　　　when I want to leave my addictions behind.
the freeway is slow on days like these,
　　　　as if we'll all forgotten the joy
of a day off of school,
a chance for forgiveness, the promise of what
　　　　a fresh start might hold.

hard candy

I'm not sure if this is penance or
poetry but I can't
keep my fists from
opening and
letting these words slip out of
my mouth I'm

sorry

for the fissures I
carved into your skin I'm
sorry

that I didn't tell you all the things you needed
to hear so that you wouldn't leave I'm

sorry
I spent thousands of
nights staring at the weight of
my insecurities
holding up the ceiling.

I'm sorry.

but you,
you
were the raspberry lifesaver crushed
beneath my tongue

and I'm sorry I
couldn't make you

stay

relapse

city night skylights:
orange clouds that blanket the stars.
down here on the ground
we are all just small people
trying to find our way home.

calling geese shatter
the winter hush of silence:
snow is on its way.
the cold makes everything still,
the stillness makes it colder.

in this time of snow,
candle lights, evergreens, and
branches heavy with
ice, your eyes are the brightest
draw, calling me back to you

water

3. *losing/healing*

cleansing is not easy when scattered
sediment is all I know, yet even
when a star dies, its light
lingers on: the heart of
the fire still burning
long after the flame
has gone out. I stand
in the rain and wash the
anger from my skin, watch the
muggy heat dissipate to bring in
cool night, wander through tinted
empathy and wade in the river of the
shadow lands until I find my way —
unfettered; drifter. a heartbeat of waves
on the cliffs here to remind my weary heart
that while the scars will always remain, a
a river can change its path and still reach
the destination. I'm prone to wander, to
squander my chances, to wait for the sirens
to call me out to sea, to drown in seaweed
wreathes and scattered dreams, hands
fisted in the sand, pulled away by chance, until the ocean
exfoliates the way I see myself, tears away the dragon
skin and holds out my soul stripped bare.

Scattered Pieces of Us

i.
I hid you inside
every corner of my heart—
                          until there were no hiding places
                          left.

        My mother once told me I feel things more deeply
than most; so I have to write them down. This,
                it seems, would be no exception:
                                        you
                        wrapped my heart in figure eights and cut
                            the story of our future into ice,
                        then raced me to meet it.

        (what good
is being the one to write all of the stories
                if I never got to tell the story
                        of us?)

        In stories, I wished you into every
                happy memory I had and
                        every one I was yet to make:

                                Japanese curry cradling my
                                        tongue, mingling
                                with brownsugarcinnamon
                                        coffee cake.

                        searching for the elephant rock
                                        on the trail

                ahead of everyone else, sun dripping
                                        through
                trees to light our way, kaleidoscoping

colors of idyllic
innocence.

those days,
            recreating Boxcar adventures and spy kid
            missions were the only things that
mattered,

because why should life be about anything else?

ii.
I look back and I realize my mistakes,
        so I'll say this once and never again:
                all my regrets for years went
                        right back to you.

                        It starts here: ski slopes that
                should also be shrouded in sun,
        fresh cut crystal mountaintops echoing
as you call me to follow you down;

instead comes the smell of the clouds,
    dark smoke shadows the sky, cutting in—we'll never
                                        be the same.
            The silence of the mountain silences us.
                        but
iii.
if we were my OTP,
                did that make me a fangirl
                        or a narcissist? Because all I wanted
                was to dance with you again so the stars
                        would shine for us—

                until you told me:
            "I don't know what to talk about
            with people I already know."

iv.
These words are the only truth I can give
        but to you, it's just lies.
             we would've bar-hopped the stars,

                and melted into pieces of sand,

           if only you'd given us a chance,
                there was a time when I would've
                followed you all the way home,
                just to warm my hand in yours
                again:
v.
instead, I fill my colorful postbox of apathy
        with memories to mail away, use my alarm
        clock to forget you ever called me friend,
             stop reliving our dance on that charming tile
—from Burger King to Pictionary to the night of prom,
        it's always just been inside my head.

vi.
So if today my hands have to crumble
        for you to know that I cared, *Que je vois*
                la vie en rose, I'll try to
            forget how
        the cups in the cupboard cried
           when I realized I loved you,
           (because I knew you'd never feel the same)

and I'll glide my ice skates through
        woodlands, down mountains, in dreams
           of the past, the present, the future,

           toward something beautifully new.

disillusionment

we were a flat tire on
the side of a two lane highway
fixable, probably, but
too far from town to be able
to go for help without some of
the magic wearing off.
There was no crash, not really,
no visible injuries, just the road
stretched out before us
our journey cut short too soon.
The only scars we'll walk away
with line up with the scuff marks
on the pavement. I didn't tell you
what I needed to
before it was too late,
but then again
neither did you.
These cornfields don't hold monsters
but they do hold secrets:
this time, they'll keep yours.
I'll wait, suspended in the fading
sunset for you to return
and wonder if you ever will.

broken mélange

empress of the day you left,
falling hard
into millions of lights,
a screen of stars
all mashed together,
silence
sirens
screaming.

empress of the empty room
a blank
pattern
following
me to the repeats of
leaflets scattered in the desk drawer.

i no longer own a desk drawer.

empress of floor corners
and night hallways
patience snuck between
computer keys and fingerprints
hull rusting, rise to
the base of the ceiling
where paperclips make their mark.

Resonant Dissonance

There is lavender by the
      poplar tree,
          the drip
              drip
                    drip
of timid afternoon
musings,
      kitten-soft on the hardening
         clay of reality.
but hollow
      echoes
         of dissonant dreams
still fog the once bright hopes
         (and thoughts),
         now encumbered by the ragged
         bog of impending truth.

this light: too harsh,
      too bright for darkening spirit,
         content instead to lie still in the cool,
      clear
                 water,
         soothing old wounds,
            until memories turn warm
         again
             until fall leaves turn
         crisp

         again
         and bring the
            bearer home.

leftovers

i.
love-lace lost in
wintry habitat, unsuspecting
mourning doves,

ransacked pieces of the
open flame. "come,"
she says to me, written across
the side of mountains,

strewn beneath the coffee grounds
scattered around the
kitchen floor.
photographs tacked on
bedroom walls.

an empty water glass
beside the empty shoes.

ii.
use this silt to tell my fortune
and maybe I'll believe
I'm more than rudiment

splattered
at the bottom
of a ceramic well

iii.
splinters of a rough-hewn
marketplace; warped individuals

in taciturn tundra
alabaster tile curded

with the cream cheese pastries
on dregs of river water.

wishing (wounding)

imagine

twinkling bugs in the field
that stretch for miles all around:
we stare at the sky,

hiding feelings in red wine,
lie on the hot grass
and recite memorized lines

of fond memories
that slip away to the stars.
hand me a full cup,

drink to those days left behind.
your fingers slip back,
but the neighbor kids call out,
break through the stardust.

I let go: you let me go.
I do not think you'll come back.

not the end

i.
biggest, best marble lost
in the north woods
of Michigan, tucked
beneath a table
somewhere.
his Boy cries
as the van drives away,
snow caught between
branches.

petty words are of
little consolation
to him: it is
the end of his world
with the marble in it.

ii.
faded red porch steps
lead me back
to Friday mornings, caught
between the sunrise
and a cup of coffee.
submarine cereal bowls
are not complete without
a blanket cape.

I leave pieces of my heart
tucked into sock drawers
and Pokémon card
collections, woven into
inscriptions scribbled on a
book page, scattered across
the
coffee table—under a
candle stuck to the wood,
beside Lego men armies.

freckled promises
are of little consolation
to me: I don't want
this to be the end
of my world
with you in it.

ex-something (ex-almost)

When it rains, I go outside
and think of you.
I didn't love you right –
whispering in my living room
in the middle of the night
so we didn't wake anyone up.
We were kicked out of the park
with a shared sorbet, and I wonder
if you still have the spoons
we bought with it at walmart because
there were no open ice cream shops.
I was afraid of getting caught:
as if I should be ashamed of
something that brought me
so much life. I'm still afraid,
of what I've lost by hiding
my true self away, these
internalized judgements pave
the way only for anger. but I'm not
angry anymore – at myself, or at you –
only at the world, at those that try,
even still, to silence us. Someday,
I will fly my colors proudly:
but today I'll wish I kissed you
beneath the glow of the capitol–
had the courage to hold your hand,
and got to dance with you,
at least once, in the rain.

torn sheets

they say to write from the scar
not the wound but when
it comes to you i have
hemophilia
a jagged piece of my heart
that never wants to stop weeping
you are the ghost that haunts
the closet
in my attic, i can
hear you rattling around
at night i wish you'd just come out,
have a cup of tea,
say the things
you want to say to me
(maybe then we both could sleep)
maybe then i'd find the words too
instead of hiding in the pantry,
a forgotten easter egg wishing
they'd find me out
so i didn't have to bleed alone

Midnight Tea

when silence rears her weathered, lonely head,
I'll slip inside the kettle on the stove
above the burning muffin treasure trove
filled with fragments from shattered, sleepless bed
frame, doused with worn out quilted clothing, burned
red from steeping in the hottest brew, the grove
of pumpkins on the shelf, in the alcove,
simmer from the shattered sunbeam's yellow thread
until the evening slips away, and hope
of moonlight serenades are written on
the sky. I'll find my fill of cleaning soap
and wash away the empty denouement
make room for patterns, puzzles, and the scope
of thoughts and words, until I see the dawn.

galaxies, and such

in the water of evening, memories vanish:
leaving spaces between the stars,
                    shooting stars,
        that we used to catch on our tongues,
                little droplets of heaven,
                        echoes of heaven,
        fitting them into the backs of our throats
        to save for a restless day.

when we were young, we ate plastic grapes
that never ran out or went dry,
        built castles on clouds
                where fairies play,
        and tucked foxes inside baskets meant
                for berry picking,
        our sailboat set on course for Neverland:
                soaring beyond the edge of the sky.

you wanted to become the galaxy,
mapping the night sky on
                the backs of your hands
        the quasar in your chest sending
        nebulae scattering from your fingertips:
I wanted to shrink to the size of a pea
        just so I could crawl under the covers
                and go back to sleep for a while.

these days, I reside in the shadowlands,
        the spaces behind wet pavement
you wait until it rains to wash your hair,
just so you can come outside
                to say hello.
        darling, slip into the shadows for a while,
    and dance with me among the stardust
                until the morning comes.

59

wine

4. (releasing) letting go

vulnerability
is a foreign
drink that
I'm terrified
to serve:
instead I
wrap my
self in
packing
paper to
store up
on the
highest shelf,
out of the way,
hidden from view,
spend my life molding
my cup into whatever you want
it to be, worried about taking up
space that someone else might need
But. Vines in the vineyard do not
worry about growing in one direction
or the other, they simply set down roots
and grow, intertwined, unafraid to offer
their fruit So: pull my heart down, polish
and set her out, glistening, dark and beautiful
red, reflecting the light, sparkling, ready to
toast in the new year–this new life– this
new me, build myself a community on
common ground where drink and bread
flows easy, where the earth is soft and
bountiful, letting out her harvest so
we can survive, surviving so that
we can thrive

hope(full)

I have strung myself out across the muted sienna sky,
fingertips murmuring in the hush of night.

Snowfall.
Silence.

Clouds wrap the earth in gentle embrace.
We pulse against them, breathing slow
and steady, heartbeat of chaos settling

into its bed. I keep the blinds open.
Noise dissipates, absorbed into the vapor.

I breathe easily here.
This nimbostratus barrier is a blanket fort
built to keep our stories safe.

The monsters under the bed
will wait for another night.

Same Hat

she stands across the tracks from me,
waiting for a different line,
I don't feel quite myself today,
but she sees me anyway. It's intrinsic
this connection—you know
the lines of framework in my brain,
a snapchat taken on a whim.
so let's be brave, let's fight the lies,
and learn to be ourselves inside.

dreams

this is the stuff that
dreams
are made of:

stardust and
        sand dunes and
              rain.

split / reality

smoke from cigarettes
lingers in the chilly air
the scent trapped in rain

wet and dry pavement
a patchwork of broken steps,
all headed somewhere

oranges in autumn
tart and sweet, finally fresh
winter is coming

a leaf on the ground
makes way for new life, the first
of many to come

streetlamp song

paper cranes and salted
memories, rose water lemonade
lined with
miscellaneous mugs, tucked
into a bankers box.

the stale perfume of
cigarette smoke and skin
shatters
marbled from winter clouds.

cups in my cupboard fill
with aluminum wine
and tassajara bread,
ravenswood
and winter ale, before the snow.

bloom

some days, it's ok
to just
be.

the water ripples. the grass rustles.
I stand in the sun,
in the smell of fallen leaves,
and remind myself:

in order to become,
I have to first exist—

like
flowers,
beside the lake, that
insist on growing,

even though
we dub them
weeds.

Barcelona

Boats in the harbor
cast longing glances at those
headed out to sea,
bright sails against a blue sky.

My hunger does not
abate in the humid air:
feet rush too quickly
to the end of the boardwalk,
stalls of fruit and fish
and candy and souvenirs.

Bikers and walkers,
Gaudi, museums, La Rambla
I keep memories
like this tucked away until
I see you again.

This city is not my home:
with you, my friend,
another could be.

persevere

history hides
between these stones,
lost to the earth
and the passing seasons,
one last monument
to life.
stories stretching into
the night, birds
and trees undisturbed
by this final resting place.
the sun still shines,
the squirrels still run,
and we will keep on,
and on and on.

for a season

ink marks and memories,
splattered and strung across a room
with glass walls, prayers and
poetry emptied into the crystal
vulnerability of a sudden

stand up dream. Our lives play out—
typed and handwritten, novels
and plays, words of success
bringing us home, crushed
between the flowers and the pages

of a well-loved book,
pressing promises onto the
tips of our fingers, held out
with our waiting hearts
we are all welcome here:

cold chairs and warm smiles
surrounded by the passion we share
by the presence of holiness, by
the spirit of peace contained
so we can learn how to show

our secrets, learn to be free.
We write, we laugh, we love.
One day, we leave, but the
life built here will always
speak hope in remembering

hope

there are galaxies
in the chasms of her eyes,
split by yearning desire
to soak up the entire world,
patterns painted into a
canopy of leaves
overhead.
we are unmoored.
waiting in the middle of a
promise, treading ground,
getting nowhere, yet: but at least
we've stopped ourselves
from drowning.
oh. listen
to the sounding sea.
my love, listen, as you roam.
listen to the heartbeat
of the universe,
and let it bring you home.

persona, personified.

she knows
everything about me:
lies of my childhood recklessness
etched into her fingers, white lines
that don't fade away:
carelessness of my teenage exuberance
rough on the bottom of her left foot,
pain of my anxious young adulthood
forever patterned across her ribs.
she knows
the taste of my blood,
the smell of my shame
as I wake, hungry, at 3 am.
she has been patient for so long, waiting on the sidelines
as neurons ricochet like a foosball
back and forth inside my skull: I am my intellect,
my thoughts, my knowledge, my faith.
nothing more.

she waits.

but.
but what if?
what if my hands are just as good, strong
and capable, the rattling lungs in my chest are perfect,
keeping me, her, us alive.
on the corner of head and heart, I stand,
waiting for my body to explain
to teach, to unite, to understand.
I am not afraid of falling.
skin dances into the early evening,
sweating, breathing, laughing,
plastic disk in the air,
sun hot, breeze cool.

she cannot run forever: but in this moment,
she will. For me, she will.
for me, she will do anything.

maybe today I'll learn to throw my heart open
like windows on a cool summer night,
and let her back in.
Maybe today, I'll learn how to
love myself again.

give and take

in June, I start to fall again
and there are sweet peaches
in the grocery store, calling my name.

I don't buy them yet: a little self-inflicted
delay of gratification is good,
sometimes.

I default to hesitation,
some might call it indecision,
unnecessary suffering, for the sake

of being sure.
But I am sure, of how I feel about her.
I am not sure how she will—

when she knows my deepest,
brightest secrets. (I am not sure
how they will either, when they learn

about these parts of me
that they were taught to hate. But,
purple clouds still burn orange

with the last rays of golden
shimmering sun.
Light trembles

on the underside
of the upside-down peaks,
reaching in vain for the

yellowed sky beneath
as it slips away, leaving behind
deep blue blankets settling

around the buttered horizon,
coaxing the tundra beneath
into gentle rest. I will write

metaphor
after metaphor,
poem after poem

in an attempt to understand
my soul:
in an attempt to explain.

vision

earth, keeper of my bones,
cool dirt spread
        beneath bare feet,
hand in hand, wandering.
we'll grow together,
                in the ebb and flow,
green life pressed to keep between our palms.

water gathers in celebration,
cloth to skin as clouds to sky—
sun-shed horizon,
        gray and tender
wraps this gentle place
in joy. two souls
forever laced in harmony.

little blue house

on the corner, autumn
leaves and petrichor
in the morning, slanted
bedroom ceilings
and slanted light.
handmade quilts tangled

into steam, rising
from mugs.
a walk through the
fog and meadow,
a picket fence that
isn't yet painted white,

leaves piling up.
Paint the sky with
gold and mist
so that this moment
will last, stitched into
every wish I have

for me and you.

at the end,

find me by the sea.
bury me in the coffers
of the waves blown back,
beneath cliffs trembling
on the shore.
craggy clouds and
rolling trees, rocks and earth
and salty sea,
a watery womb that waxes
and wanes

let the waves embrace
my weary skin.
my bones rejoice with
seaweed wreaths. the
torment is over: we shall be
free—for evening
is spread and waiting.
it's everything we could want,
scattered
throughout the world enough.
and time, love, is left
for the taking.

NOTES

cups in the cupboard is an homage to my past and an ode to my future. This collection has been a long time coming, and includes poetry written between 2014 and 2024. Since it took me 10 years to write, many of the early themes and feelings are ones I have left in years gone by, though they will always be a part of me in some way.

I hope that I have accurately conveyed a small part of my journey: from an anxious kid (yearning for something she couldn't quite explain) to a hopeful adult (much less afraid of the future or of being true to herself). Feelings are complicated and don't always make sense, but it gets better, I promise.

If you find yourself experiencing feelings of depression or anxiety, or are suicidal, please seek help. There are so many people that love you.

Notes on the Four Sections:

Coffee = Longing, Hurting.
Anxiety, and anxious longing. Longing for someone to love, uncertainty of self. Deep insecurity.

Tea = Loving, Bleeding.
Depression. Trying to love and failing. Trying to express it. Loving, unreciprocated. Love that falls apart, for no good reason at all. The hard part.

Water = Losing. Healing.
Losing love, losing past identities of self. Losing things, but for the better. Growing into a stronger, more capable person. Understanding more of life. Healing from past hurt.

Wine = Letting Go.
Letting go and moving forward. Taking the past into consideration, using it to grow, but not letting it fester any longer. Finding hope and reaching for better things.

ACKNOWLEDGEMENTS

A big thank you to all my English teachers over the years (including you, Mom!), without whom I never would have discovered, explored, and developed my lifelong love of poetry.

Extra special thanks to Kristy Odelius, for providing prompts, feedback, and encouragement for many of these poems written between 2014 and 2017.

To my parents and sister, for always being there for me.

To Sara, for being my ride or die.

To Meagan and Hannah, for reading and editing this manuscript, and for your unwavering belief and support.

To those I have loved and lost, but especially to those that have stayed.

To everyone who's ever asked to read my work, or expressed interest when I told them I'm writing a book of poetry.

And to you, the reader, for making it this far.

ABOUT THE AUTHOR

Clarissa R. Sutton starting writing at a very young age and never stopped. While studying for a BA in English, she discovered an even deeper love of all kinds of storytelling, and poetry as a form of self-expression was born. Some of her poetry has been previously published in *The North Branch Literary Journal* in 2016 and 2017. She views poetry is a way to express the inexpressible, through metaphor and observation of the world around her. When she's not writing, Clarissa can be found in nature, daydreaming about a different project than the one she should be working on, or getting her naughty cat out of places he shouldn't be. She currently lives in Iowa, with said cat.

@clarissarsutton
www.crsutton.com